written and illu

from the darkest night

meditations for abuse survivors

written and illustrated by Melanie Jansen

from the darkest night
meditations for abuse survivors

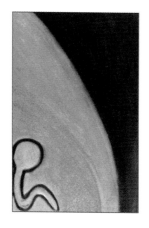

FAITH
ALIVE®
Christian Resources

Grand Rapids, Michigan

Faith Alive Christian Resources published by CRC Publications.
From the Darkest Night: Meditations for Abuse Survivors, © 2001 by CRC Publications, 2850 Kalamazoo Ave. SE, Grand Rapids, MI 49560. All rights reserved. With the exception of brief excerpts for review purposes, no part of this book may be reproduced in any manner whatsoever without written permission from the publisher. Printed in the United States of America on recycled paper. ♻

We welcome your comments. Call us at 1-800-8300 or e-mail us at editors@faithaliveresources.org.

Library of Congress Cataloging-in-Publication Data
Jansen, Melanie, 1963–
    From the darkest night: meditations for abuse survivors / written and illustrated by Melanie Jansen.
      p. cm.
    ISBN 1-56212-543-5
      1. Adult child abuse victims--Prayer books and devotions--English.
        I. Title.
BV4596.A25 J36 2001
242'.4--dc21

                                                2001033687

10 9 8 7 6 5 4 3 2 1

To Kevin Franke, with gratitude.

CONTENTS

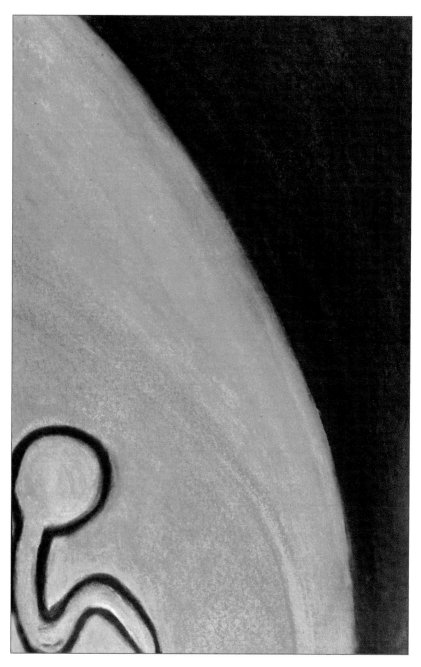

The sense of isolation I felt for many years
was profound and impenetrable.

Introduction

When I first started thinking about writing these meditations, I wondered what I would have to say that you or any other survivor would want to read. But one of the truths I face every day is that I have survived. And I am continuing to survive. These meditations are not intended as a self-help guide to show you the way to healing. I do not have some special knowledge that will magically take away your pain. I am simply one survivor who wants to share with others some of the morsels that helped keep me alive—physically and spiritually—while I was on my own lonely journey.

In the long run, you must find your own way to healing. Not because you are alone but because you are a unique person, and what helps one person doesn't necessarily help another. One person's path to healing is not everyone's path. Only you know and God knows (even if it doesn't seem so right now) how to find your path to healing. Other people may come and walk part of the way with you. Perhaps you'll even find someone who will walk all the way with you. Either way, it's my hope that this collection of meditations will serve as a walking stick to help you through some of the difficult parts of the path.

As you have already noticed, I talk about God in these meditations—not a "higher power" or "that which leads you on" or "the light." That's because I understand the Being who created me, who loves me, and who counts the hairs on my head as God. You might not. Maybe you feel an understandable aversion or anger toward God. If that's true for you, I encourage you to substitute whatever name makes you feel most comfortable while you are reading these meditations. The name is not important; the Being is.

Over the years, I have drawn a great deal of strength from reading the Bible. At times, reading the Bible was the last thing I wanted to do, and so I didn't. But I have found that when I can read the Bible without the voices of my childhood running through my head—when I can read it with innocent eyes, so to speak—then I can hear a message of love. And from that message of love I draw my strength.

It's true that the Bible includes some horrific passages that paint a grim picture of human life. But I believe that the Bible, taken as a whole, has one underlying theme: God wants to be in relationship with me. And with you.

I have closed each of these meditations with a Celtic prayer. These prayers have been particularly helpful during those times when I have been unable to talk with God. I've also discovered that they carry no baggage—these are words I can use to express my hope, as a true prayer for the things I yearn for. For me they have been a small but significant declaration of my own power and ability to ask for what I needed during a time when getting what I needed seemed impossible.

The pictures that illustrate this volume are mine. I drew them in the depths of my struggle. They helped me affirm the reality of my experience as well as illustrate my pain. Many people have commented that they are "beautiful"—they are not so in my eyes. But I have learned that my pain can sometimes be transformed into something of value to another. I hope that is so once more.

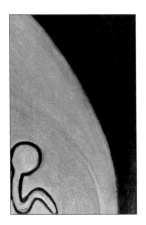

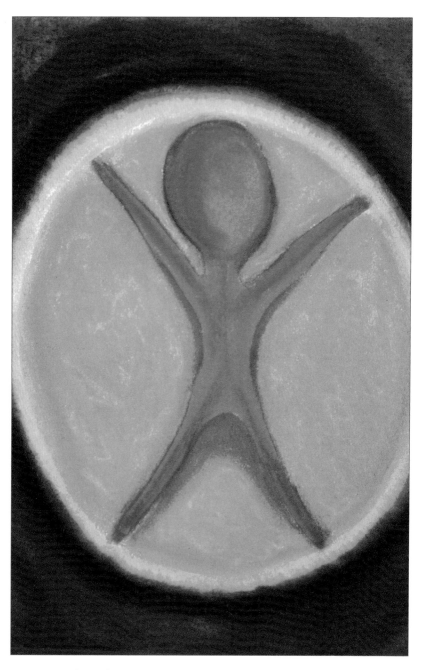

The web created by my experience contrasts strongly with Leonardo da Vinci's study of perfect proportions. This image shows that I was far from a position of balance. In fact, I felt extremely cut off from God.

Where Was God?

Why, O LORD, do you reject me and hide your face from me?
—**Psalm 88:14**

Where was God when you were suffering? That's a tough question, one that's been around for a long time—back to the time of the psalm writers and before. If you are a survivor, the question seems inescapable. Where was God while I was being abused? Why didn't God protect me from being raped, beaten, threatened, terrorized, and neglected? How could the Being who spent so much energy creating me, who knit me together in my mother's womb, allow someone to hurt me so badly? Where was God?

And that question leads to another: Where *is* God? If God wasn't there when I was a child, when I was weak and unprotected, how can I believe that God is here now that I am grown, and more powerful? What kind of God shows up when I don't need help and neglects me when I do? And what do I need with a God like that? More tough questions.

In a conversation with a chaplain friend about my experience of abuse, he commented, "You know, if I were you, I would have to conclude that God wasn't there."

God wasn't there? How could that be? I had always been told that God was everywhere, watching out for me. As a child, I had sung songs that reassured me that God was up above, looking over me. Now a man of God was suggesting that God wasn't there for me in those circumstances. Unthinkable.

After this conversation, I started paying attention to the people in the Bible whom God had apparently abandoned. The crucifixion scene jumped immediately to mind. Jesus said it straight from the heart: "My God, my God, why have you forsaken me?" (Matt. 27:46). Noah, confined inside the ark for over a year, with death and destruction all around him, also must have felt pretty far away from God. And where was God while Bathsheba's husband, Uriah, was being murdered? God certainly didn't protect him. The Bible is filled with examples of people who seem to have been abandoned by God.

And so the unthinkable isn't so unthinkable after all. There are times when God is apparently absent. My experience as a child cut off from the protecting hand of God is reflected over and over again in the Bible. And perhaps it's reflected in your life too, or in the lives of your friends.

I don't know. I don't know where God is *right now*. I believe that God is everywhere, but I don't have empirical evidence to back that up. I can't prove the presence of God even when I feel it. And I certainly don't know where God is when the only ones present are me or you and the horror that is happening to us.

Our perspective, however, is limited. We can see a house across the street. But we cannot see what is behind the house. We cannot see around corners. We cannot observe the sun shining on the other side of the earth in the middle of our night. Even so, we know that the sun is still burning in space and that the people on the other side of the earth can see it. They see that which we cannot see.

In a similar way, we are sometimes unable to feel the presence of God. During those times, God is not there for us. We feel left alone.

Perhaps this seems like a cop-out. After all, if the problem is really with our perception—if God really is with us but we can't feel God's presence during certain times of our lives—then something must be wrong with us. Maybe you think that God wasn't there while you were getting hurt because you didn't have enough faith to see him. But what kind of comfort is that?

The truth is, sometimes there isn't any comfort. Some questions have no easy answers. Sometimes there are just tough answers, or no answers at all. You know this; I know it.

Still, absolutely nobody on this earth has the power or the ability or the gift of feeling the presence of God all the time or even most of the time. Being human necessarily means that we are limited. And those of us who have been severely hurt by other people are further limited.

This is the hard part. This is where belief enters. You must believe. You must trust, sometimes without any hard evidence at all, in the presence of God. The Bible promises that God will be with us. Not a hair falls from our head without God knowing about it. God is with you after all. God cares for you. God knows you inside and out. Will you feel God's presence? Maybe. Will you see God? Maybe, and maybe not.

Knowing our limitations, God gives us a gift to help us see. The people who love you and care for you become the place to find God when God seems absent. The people around you are the ones who can see the sun shining in the middle of your night: your therapist, friend, roommate, partner, spouse, child, doctor, dentist, mechanic, bus driver, neighbor, or mail carrier. Anybody who brings light and life into your life marks the presence of God.

Sometimes you have to believe in order to see. And sometimes belief is all you have.

Lord from this world's stormy sea

Give your hand for lifting me

Lord lift me from the darkest night

Lord lift me into the realm of light

Lord lift me from this body's pain

Lord lift me up and keep me sane

Lord lift me from the things I dread

Lord lift me from the living dead

Lord lift me from the place I lie

Lord lift me that I never die.

Some days I felt that getting well would cause me to split apart. During the period of time I was drawing these pictures, the color blue represented lies and deception.

Relearning the Lessons

Then a voice told him, "Get up, Peter. Kill and eat."

"Surely not, Lord!" Peter replied. "I have never eaten anything impure or unclean."

The voice spoke to him a second time, "Do not call anything impure that God has made clean."
—**Acts 10:13-15**

Living is much harder than dying. I found that out when I was working my hardest to stay alive in the face of crushing depression and hopelessness. It would have been easier to give up—to kill myself or just allow myself to die. I didn't think the world ought to work this way. Living should be easy and dying difficult, not the other way around.

Muddling through this conundrum made me wonder if I had gotten it all wrong. What if what I thought was true *wasn't* true, and what if what I didn't believe *was* true? This nagging question caused me to rethink many things I had believed. I'd believed that I should never have been born. I believed that, having been born, I didn't deserve to live. I believed that my life was not my own, that it belonged either to my family or to my abusers or to God or to anyone who asked for it.

Back to the drawing board. I started pondering the reality of my birth. If God really created me, knit me together in my mother's womb, counted the hairs on my head, and sent Jesus to die on the cross for me, then maybe I was worth something after all. God didn't go through all that work of creating me just to let me suffer and die. So I had to choose: either believe in a God who loved me and wanted me to be happy, or believe in no God at all. I chose to believe in the God who loved me. Sometimes faith means you just have to make a choice and go with it.

This idea that God loved me upset all my false beliefs. I had believed that I was to make other people happy, that they could do with me what they wanted, that I was too fat, too smart, too intro-verted, too loud, too tactless, too bookish, too angry. Whatever I was, I was too much of it. And not one bit of me was lovable. I believed that anything good in me had been destroyed or stolen through the act of being abused. There was nothing good left.

I needed to relearn so many things! Although I didn't recognize it at the time, I needed to become a disciple. I needed to turn away from one life and commit to another. I had to discipline myself to embrace a new philosophy and learn a new way of life.

Like the disciple Peter, I needed to unlearn what I used to think was true. A time came in Peter's life when God told him to eat food he considered unclean: "Go ahead, Peter. Eat it, even though you've never eaten it before." Peter must have wondered if God had gone a little crazy. After all, eating unclean food would break a funda-mental law that governed Peter's life. In Peter's time, much of Jewish life focused on the rituals surrounding eating: what to eat, how to prepare it, when to eat what. So this notion from God—"Don't call anything bad that I have created"—turned Peter's world upside down, just as it turned mine upside down.

God created life; God created me. Believing both of these things, how could I continue to call either one impure, burdensome, things to be shunned? And yet, a large stone of my life's foundation was based on my belief that I was "unclean." I wanted to reject myself. I struggled and still struggle with seeing myself as God does. Every day, despite my best efforts, I dishonor the person God created me to be.

I have to accept what I now believe to be true: I am good because God created me. At first this idea so disoriented me that I felt like I was walking on the ceiling of an upside-down room. But I came to believe in that goodness despite all the evil that had been done to me.

I continually have to tell myself that I am not a reflection of that evil. I have been given the gift of life, and God rejoices every time I reach out or open up enough to receive it. I don't need to live a narrow life, eating only certain foods, experiencing only the sad parts of life. I can choose to receive all the good things that God has created.

All of this requires discipline. I must fight to defeat the devils that plague me, the voices that tell me over and over again that I am worth nothing, that life must be full of sadness and that I was born only to suffer. Sometimes I am able to silence those voices, and sometimes not. Sometimes discipline takes the form of just plain stubbornness. On days when I hit bottom, I tell myself that if I give up, the bad guys win. If I don't make it, the people who abused me have triumphed. And I am simply not going to let that happen.

You know the voices of your own demons. They tell you that you deserve your suffering, that you are being punished for something wrong in your life. They may be relentless. Remind yourself that they are speaking lies. Remind yourself that you deserve to be loved, even if you have done terrible things you regret.

Once you have lived with death, it is incredibly difficult to find the joy of life. But it is possible. The steps to the place of joy are small. They may seem endless. But the climb out of death is possible.

I have come to believe that God has given me the gift of life to enjoy. I know now that the sufferings I have experienced are not of God's doing. They are the work of evil forces in the world. Staying out of the pit of death is a daily struggle. But I no longer believe that I don't deserve life. I deserve it because God gave it to me.

Glory to God on earth peace

Let this song never cease.

As I arise this morn

Christ in me be born

When I wash my face

Bless me with your grace

When I comb my hair

Keep me from despair

When I put on my clothes

Your presence Lord disclose

Glory to God on earth peace

Let this song never cease.

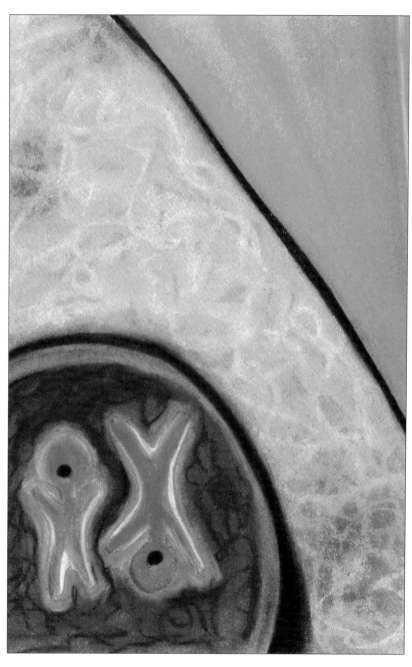

There were often two of me: the skin I lived in,
and the one who told me falsehoods and
worked very hard to keep me from the truth.

THREE
The Pharisee Syndrome

For everyone who exalts himself will be humbled, and he who humbles himself will be exalted.

—Luke 18:14

I had to practice learning how to trust. First I had to pretend to trust, which made me feel a little silly—after all, I was almost thirty years old. Pretending to trust was very much like playing house: I'm going to be the mother and I'm going to take care of you. You are going to be the baby. Go lie down over there. I was the mother and the baby at the same time.

The first time I pretended to trust someone was when I went out for lunch with a woman I had known for quite some time. She had always treated me in a kind and caring way, so I thought I would practice pretending to trust her first. I thought about how I might act if I trusted her. Since I had no instinct for trusting, I based all my actions on what people had told me were the things people did when they trusted each other. We had a very nice lunch together while I pretended to trust her.

I found out that learning to trust is much harder work than I thought it was going to be. Pretending to trust is one thing; continuing to trust is another thing altogether.

According to the dictionary, *trust* means "a firm belief in the reliability or truth or strength of a person or thing, a confident expectation." Trust involves believing that someone or something is what it appears to be. My experience, on the other hand, had taught me otherwise—the people who had appeared to care for me had hurt me severely instead. When I think about that experience, I can forgive myself for having so much difficulty trusting. After all, the "confident expectation" I learned as a child was that people would hurt me.

The first thing I found out about myself when I was learning to trust was that my shoulders needed to drop down an inch or two. Apparently I had been walking around with my shoulders up by my ears most of the time. Even now I have to remind myself that I do have a neck, as I drop my shoulders once more.

So why should I learn to trust? Because I have discovered that not trusting people (or only trusting them a small amount) requires me to believe a lie. What is the lie? That if only I could do everything right—follow all the rules, obey the laws—then I would be OK. What's more, if I had followed the rules, the horrible things that happened to me would not have happened.

You see, I believed that I had been hurt because I had done something wrong. Maybe I'd been hurt because I'd been too attractive. Maybe I'd been abused because I didn't tell anyone about it; I didn't act like I was suffering, so no one knew.

Because my trust was betrayed in a fundamental way, I built a large portion of my life on the foundation of betrayal. I spent many years trying to be good in an effort to undo the betrayal of trust I had experienced. I believed that if I followed the rules I could somehow cancel out what had happened and prevent it from happening again. If I acted in all the right ways, then everything would be all right.

But you know and I know that life doesn't work that way. One of the reasons people are abused is because they don't have enough power to defend themselves. Abuse doesn't have anything to do with whether or not we do the right things or follow all the rules. And that is one of the reasons it hurts so much.

The ultimate biblical example of someone who follows all the rules has got to be the Pharisee in the story of the Pharisee and the tax collector (Luke 18:9-14). The Pharisee stood in the temple praying loudly for everyone to hear, doing everything exactly right, sure that he had a place in heaven. In the corner stood the tax collector, taking nothing for granted, just grateful to be in the temple at all.

This story is partly about what kind of control we think we have. The Pharisee believes that if he says his prayers, obeys the law, and gives to the poor, he will be welcomed into the kingdom of heaven. The tax collector has no such illusion. He is completely convinced that he has little control over his fate. He is grateful for the life he has. He says his prayers because he wants to talk to God, not because he wants to ensure a place in heaven.

I'm more like the Pharisee. Like him, I love the idea of following all the rules and being rewarded for it. What could possibly be better? But now I understand that following the rules does not necessarily make good things happen. And I can't undo what has been done. I didn't get hurt because I did something wrong, or because I was attractive or willing or naïve or silent. My behavior—whether perfect or imperfect—would not have made one bit of difference.

Why learn to trust? To break the lie that I could have done something to change what happened.

As a child, I believed I had some kind of control over my life, but I obviously didn't. I couldn't choose where to live or what to eat. I had no say in where I went to school or who was in my class. No one consulted me about who was to have power over my life and who wasn't.

As an adult, I didn't think I had any choices except to obey all the rules, but now I've learned that I have the power to make choices. I don't have to do what people tell me to do. I don't have to be what they want me to be. I do not have to please everyone to be happy.

Finally, I can choose to let some people into my life and not others. I am learning that not all people are dangerous, and that some people—but not all—can be trusted.

Thy Presence come between me

And all things evil

Thy Presence come between me

And all things vile

Thy Presence come between me

And all things of guile

Thy Presence come between me

And all things that defile

Keep me O Lord as the apple of thine eye

Hide me under the shadow of thy wings.

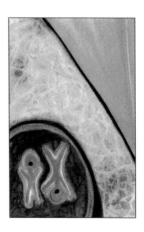

During my journey toward healing, being in church
often made me feel that I was being sacrificed.

What About Church?

But a Samaritan, as he traveled, came where the man was; and
when he saw him, he took pity on him. He went to him and
bandaged his wounds, pouring on oil and wine. Then he put the
man on his own donkey, took him to an inn and took care of him.
—Luke 10:33-34

I used to go to church every Sunday. I dressed up for Sunday serv-
ices, came on time, and stayed through Sunday school. I joined
committees and led the high school youth group. I was the ideal
church member—the kind most churches would love to have.

But when I started dealing with childhood abuse, my relationship
to church changed. I found I couldn't bear to sit in a church. I
couldn't tolerate being with Christians who were praising God. For
that matter, I couldn't stand being with a group of Christians in any
setting. People who called themselves Christians had abused me;
other Christians had failed to help. With the weight of my experience pressing on me, Christianity became a religion of hypocrites.
I didn't want any part of it.

Church can be a big problem for people who have been abused.
And coping with people who have been abused can be a big problem for the church. That's because, like most people, Christians find
it hard to look at the presence of evil in their lives or in the lives of
the people around them. We expect Christians to be experts at car-

ing for the sick and the wounded, but that's not always the case. Like most people, Christians tend to turn away from suffering.

Take a look at the parable of the Good Samaritan in Luke 10. A man is beaten unconscious and left lying in the road. A priest and a Levite, both in special positions of authority and relationship to God, avoid the man. Like many of us, they walk away. Jesus wasn't just making this up; he was accurately describing human nature. People of God not helping those who are hurting is an old story.

So why bother with a group of people who can't even take care of their own? Why go to church? It's certainly much easier to turn away from the church, and not attending hurts less than attending. If you're not there, you don't have to listen to comments about how God doesn't give us more than we can handle or how we just need to have more faith.

First, it's important to remember that church is not all there is to our relationship with God. Not attending church for a time doesn't mean cutting yourself off from God. Nowhere does the Bible say that God stops loving you if you don't attend church. Unless you deliberately turn your back on God, God will hold you, pursue you, love you, and forgive you. God will comfort you wherever you are. That's a promise.

You also need to remember that God and the church are not the same thing. If you have been abused by someone in the church or encouraged to stay in an abusive relationship by someone in the church, that congregation cannot embody the Spirit of God to you. In that case, it's especially important to make a distinction between the God who loves you and the church, which sometimes fails to live up to its high calling.

God can handle our feelings—even the negative ones. I have spent a good portion of my time with God expressing my anger about how I felt God failed me. How could God not have protected me? Where was God in my dark days and nights? And how can everyone around me sing the praises of this God? During the times I struggled with these questions, I very much doubted whether God cared for me. And through it all, God has never once struck me with lightning. The earth did not open up and swallow me. God has never punished me for my feelings or for expressing them.

Here is a promise worth staking your life on: God loves you. If you believe nothing else, believe this. Even if you don't feel it. Rant and rave at God about how you don't feel it. But be willing to risk believing in a loving God. If you don't feel God's love, keep at God to show it to you. Demand that God show up in your life, in your church. And then open your heart. It's worth it.

Perhaps you're stepping back here. *No thanks,* you may be thinking. *I don't need any more pain in my life.* You're right. Believing in God's love *is* painful. Lancing a boil is painful, but it also leads to healing. In the depths of my pain, I found God. I still hurt. I thought I would die, I wished I would die, I tried to die. And in all of that, God was. In my pain is where I found God. And in finding God, I started to heal.

Eventually I started to attend church again. And God was there too. God doesn't make everything happy and beautiful, and my experience of God is certainly different from what I learned as a child. But

I do know this: God stands by me and stands by me and stands by me. And by you. God knows your struggles, your hurt, your anger.

So, back to the question I asked earlier. Why go to church? In spite of the pain, I finally chose to go because I had become lonely for the incarnation of God. I yearned to hear God's Word spoken and sung. I wanted to see joy in people's faces when they talked about what God had done. I wanted to be inspired by someone else's comments about their spiritual journey. I wanted to talk about God and struggle with the questions of where God was when I was hurting. I was acting on my desire to believe again.

When I started attending church again, I cried through every service for the next year. It was painful to hear that God loved me when I couldn't feel it. It was hard to hear hymns proclaiming God as my fortress and my rock when that didn't seem to be true. I yearned to feel God's presence. And the people around me seemed to feel a comfort I was craving. It was excruciating. But slowly I began to stop hurting quite so much. I found Christians who were willing to walk the narrow path with me, friends who comforted me in my struggle. I found a place where I felt safe, where I could see God.

I believe we all have a built-in yearning for God. Our souls thirst to be reunited with God. Reach out and follow your soul's desire, and you will find God.

What can separate us from the love of God?

Can sickness or death?

No nothing can separate us from the love of God

Can danger or war?

No nothing can separate us from the love of God

Can sadness or despair?

No nothing can separate us from the love of God

Can failure or rejection?

No nothing can separate us from the love of God

Can loneliness or fear?

No nothing can separate us from the love of God

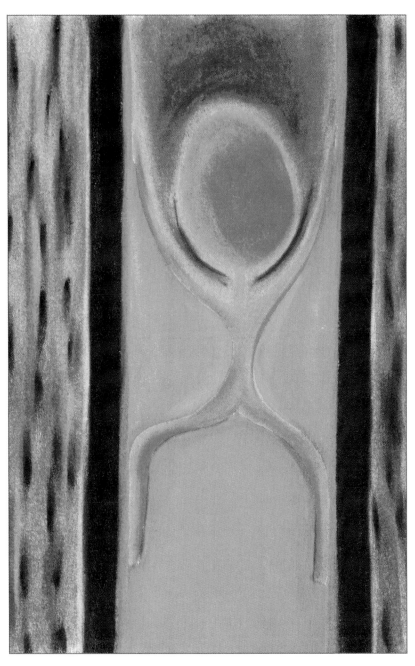

In this image a storm of tears appears on either
side of me. I was barely hanging in there.

FIVE
Healing Hurts

Why is my pain unending and my wound grievous and incurable?
—Jeremiah 15:18

Healing is painful. That's one of life's well-kept secrets, but all burn patients know it firsthand. Serious burns cause extreme pain not only in the injury but also in the healing. People with bad burns must endure a series of grafts, wrappings, soakings, and debridements. Grafting is a process in which healthy skin is cut off part of the body and transferred to the burned area. Although grafting often works well, it leaves yet another open, bleeding wound that needs to heal, adding scars to an area that was uninjured. Debridement is a process by which the dead skin is removed in one of several ways—either cut or soaked or scrubbed off—to allow new skin to form. None of this work can be done under anesthetics, so the person feels exquisitely every scrape, pull, and cut.

In some ways, healing from abuse is like recovering from a severe burn. The pain may not be physical, but it's real and severe, nonetheless.

If I ran the universe, there would be a law restricting the amount of pain any one person has to bear. Anyone who experiences pain in an injury should not have to suffer even more pain to get well. But the truth is, getting well is often incredibly painful. Why can't getting well feel wonderful? Sometimes it does. More often it doesn't.

If getting well felt good, more people would be doing it. Sickness, injury, alcoholism, workaholism, and mental illness wouldn't be so rampant if it felt really great to get well. We'd all be running around begging to be healed. Halfway houses would be empty, and therapists would be looking for new careers.

Most of us *are* longing to be healed. We might not be looking in the right places for healing, but we are yearning to be whole nonetheless. You wouldn't be reading this book if you weren't looking for healing from something.

In Scripture, people are generally healed with a minimum of fuss, and there is generally no mention of the pain and suffering that go along with it. But then, most of those healings are of the miraculous sort. And although miracles are always welcome, they aren't something we can depend on for healing all our hurts.

Where does that leave us? With the difficult daily grind of getting well. For me, healing has come in very small steps. Every little step I take feels like I am ripping off yet one more piece of dead skin so that new, healthy skin can grow in its place. Because it hurts so much, I have to pause after each step to recover. Step, rest, step, rest, rest; OK, move back a little because this far forward is too uncomfortable.

Being severely traumatized kills off parts of yourself, very important parts—the trusting part, the loving and compassionate part, the courageous part, the fun-loving part. Much of you feels dead. There isn't enough oxygen or food or love or whatever you need to be alive. So parts of you die. When you get to the point where you want to be truly alive, you have to get rid of all the dead stuff before you can grow the healthy stuff. And wow, does that hurt!

A friend of mine suggested that healing is like playing Monopoly while blindfolded. You are going around the board, buying property. Although you're gaining ground, you can't see it. Then you take off the blindfold and discover that you've just bought Park Place, and you're about to pass GO and collect $200. On my journey toward healing my friends kept telling me, "You are really doing great. You're making progress"—in other words, I had reached St. Charles Place—but I could never see it. I felt like I was still stuck at GO or, worse yet, sitting in jail with no "Get Out of Jail Free" card in sight.

So why bother to heal? Why not just stay with the pain you know instead of finding new pain? It's true that not everyone wants to get well. Lots of people think they do, but when it comes right down to it, they prefer staying in the place they know—however painful—to moving forward. I have no illusions about just how difficult it is to heal. It takes work, it is painful, and it can separate you from the things or people you love most in the world. Not everyone is able to travel that road.

I wanted to get well because I wanted to experience love. I was too dead to feel anyone's love—including God's—until I became well. But I had another powerful reason for wanting to get well: I didn't want my abusers to ruin the rest of my life. I wanted a good, fulfilling, enjoyable life—for at least part of my life.

Like me, you probably have your own reasons for wanting to be well. Yes, healing hurts. In moving toward healing, we must be willing to endure the pain of the journey. We must be willing to sacrifice our present pain for an unknown pain. Finally, we must be willing to embrace a full life with the expectation that we have a future worth living for ahead of us.

When I am sick and ill

Your health will heal me still.

Come Holy Dove

Cover with love

Spirit be about my head

Spirit peace around me shed

Spirit light about my way

Spirit guardian night and day

Come Holy Dove

Cover with love

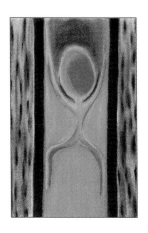

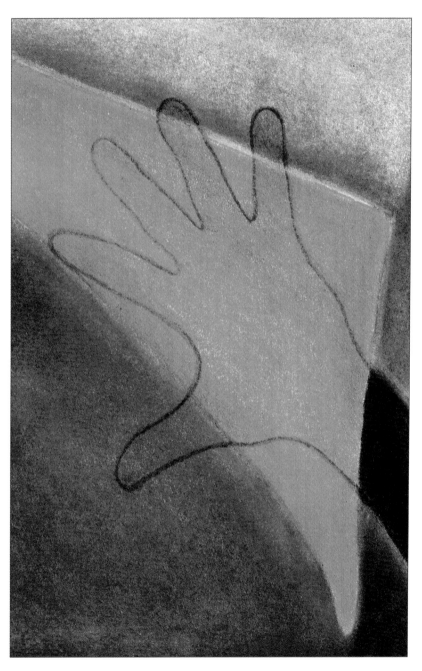

I often had the urge to smash my hands with a hammer. It is so very difficult to stop hurting.

SIX

Perpetuating the Pain

If only my anguish could be weighed and all my misery be placed on the scales!

It would surely outweigh the sand of the seas . . .

—Job 6:2-3

Once when my spiritual advisor asked me to describe my pain, I thought of a scene from a movie I had seen recently. One man is fighting another with a broadsword. Both are severely injured; they're barely able to hold their swords up, much less engage in a battle. Finally, in one last gathering of strength, the first man swings his sword over his head and brings it down on the second man's shoulder, cutting him from the base of his neck through his chest and almost to his waist.

That second person—the one cut in two—was me.

You may have your own, equally horrific picture of your pain. Because all of us know pain intimately, even if we don't show it. Sometimes our pain is so great that it becomes a way of life. For some of us, to be alive is to be in pain.

The morning after I tried to commit suicide, the psychiatric nurse asked me why I wanted to hurt myself. I wasn't trying to hurt myself, I explained, I was trying to *stop* hurting. The majority of my energy went into trying to avoid getting hurt or to avoid feeling the hurt I had already experienced. I was in agony almost all of the time. I thought I could stop the pain only by stopping my life.

In this state, I strongly identified with the woman who had a bleeding disorder for twelve years (see Mark 5:25-29). Her disease caused her to be an outcast, resulting in a kind of suffering that others couldn't easily see. Like the woman, I felt like my life force was dripping out of me every day—a draining I couldn't stop. This woman believed that she would be healed if only she could touch the hem of Jesus' robe. I too wanted to touch Jesus' robe and be healed.

One of the ways I tried to stop the draining away of my life was by hurting myself. The act of self-mutilation is one of the secrets kept by many people who have lived through severe trauma. We injure ourselves in an effort to find relief from our suffering. The pain I inflicted on myself kept me from worrying about what someone else might do to hurt me. With this pain, at least I knew it was coming.

People hurt themselves in lots of ways. Some are physical: cutting or burning, starving, binging and purging, drinking, taking drugs. Some are not physical but are just as harmful: getting into repeated abusive relationships, setting themselves up for failure at work, allowing themselves to get hurt by someone over and over again.

The self-injuring I am talking about seems unstoppable; it is literally overwhelming. It is as if someone or something has taken over your will, pushing you to hurt yourself. If you had asked me whether I had intended to hurt myself, I would have said no. Not in a million years. I was, after all, on a journey to try to *stop* hurting. In spite of that, I hurt myself over and over again, often without even noticing.

I sometimes felt like the man in the gospel of Mark who was possessed by demons. "Night and day among the tombs and in the hills he would cry out and cut himself with stones" (Mark 5:1-20). Here was a man besieged by evil, whose only logical response was to hurt himself. I knew what that was like.

Being abused had taught me that I was nothing, an object to be used. It taught me that I didn't exist except as something worth hurting. The only way I knew I was alive was to feel pain. For a long time, this was my mantra: Life is pain, and anyone who tells you different is lying.

What the church had taught me only reinforced that belief. In church I learned about giving yourself, about denying yourself in order to serve. I learned that to be like Christ I had to be willing to give up my life. Being a Christian, I believed, meant suffering. The pick-up-your-cross-and-follow-me command carried a lot of weight. To me, the Golden Rule—love your neighbor as yourself— meant loving your neighbor at the *expense* of yourself.

So how did I get from there to here? In a word, *healing.* Jesus healed both of the people I identified with—the woman hemorrhaging for twelve years and the demon-possessed man. I desperately wanted to be healed too. Although I had trouble focusing on a Jesus who suffered to the point of death, I could deal with a Jesus who chose to heal those who were suffering. That seemed like a good place to start.

I began to question some of the things I had learned as a child. I figured that if God really thought we should suffer unto death, then Jesus would not have healed the woman. He would have let her die. And he would have allowed the man to continue to suffer.

Perhaps, I reasoned, life doesn't mean just suffering after all. Maybe, and this was a big maybe for me, I could be healed.

I also began to realize that the Golden Rule has two parts: loving your neighbor, and loving yourself. You are to love your neighbor *as yourself*. Just how well did I love myself? I was hurting myself regularly. Not a very good way to love anyone, much less myself. Before I did anything else, I decided to try to learn how to love myself.

The idea of taking up your cross also faded in significance. As I started to look at how little I loved myself, I began to realize that I was already carrying a sizeable cross. I hardly needed to go looking for one elsewhere.

As I've said, nobody talks about how painful healing can be. You'd expect that beginning to feel good would feel good. But it doesn't always work that way. Mostly starting to feel good just feels bad. Especially at the beginning, when you are just learning what feeling good and loving yourself feels like. Feeling good means leaving that life of pain, a life that is all you might have known. You're in unknown territory. No markers, no road maps. It's very scary.

At that point, the irresistible urge to go back to hurting whispers in your ear all the reasons why the old familiar pain is better than the unknown. Recognize that for what it is—a lie. The pain of abuse, of self-inflicted injury, will lead you nowhere fast. But the pain of healing will lead to less pain—and eventually to healing.

The Spirit of God lives within each of us. Our bodies are holy places—not objects, not things. Holy. Pure, faultless, uncorrupt, spotless, clean. So remember this: No matter what you've suffered, God sees your body as sacred and whole.

Lord strengthen every good

Defeat the power of evil

Lord strengthen every light

Defeat the power of darkness

Lord strengthen every joy

Defeat the power of sadness

Lord strengthen every love

Defeat the power of hatred

Lord strengthen every life

Defeat the power of death

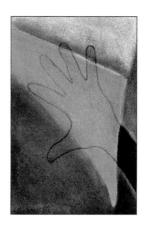

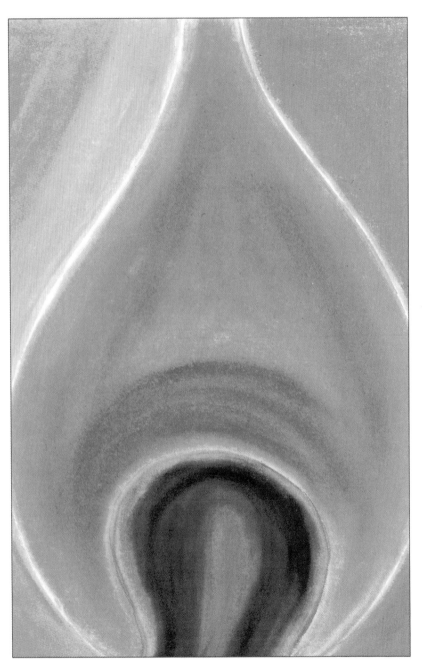

Tears were sometimes the only thing in my vision.

SEVEN
The Need for Lament

Let your tears flow like a river
day and night;
give yourself no relief,
your eyes no rest. . . .
Pour out your heart like water
in the presence of the Lord.
—Lamentations 2:18-19

When I was a child I was frequently told that I complained too much. Once, when I was nine or ten years old, I made a New Year's resolution not to complain. Of course, that went the way of most resolutions, and to this day I am still a great complainer. I've found that complaining is good for my soul. When I'm with friends, I sometimes preface my complaints with a statement of intent: "I am just complaining here." Then they know that I am not expecting them to fix what I am complaining about. And they allow me to go on as long as I need to.

Believe me—complaining can be very cathartic. Keep in mind that I'm talking here about honest expression about what's wrong in your life—not the kind of constant whining that seems to control some people. At that point, complaining becomes enslavement, not release.

Like me, you may have grown up in a culture that frowned on complaining of any sort. Unless you were dying of something, you knew you'd better suffer in silence. Even if you were dying, people would think more of you if you did it quietly and with a minimum of fuss. Expressing your suffering verbally was seen as the sign of a weak constitution, and besides, it disturbed the people around you. Even worse, complaining reflected poorly on your Christian faith. Surely, if you felt the need to vent your not-so-nice feelings about life, your relationship with God must be a bit off. The idea was that Christians ought to feel grateful to God for just about everything. A major crisis might allow for some negative comments—but certainly not a full expression of loss or sorrow. Needless to say, my gift for complaining made it impossible for me to fit in very well.

This chapter is for people like me who learned that to lament is a bad thing. I beg to differ with that idea. Scripture is full of lament. A whole book of the Bible—appropriately called Lamentations—is committed to expressions of sorrow. (You probably won't be surprised to hear that it's one of my favorite books.) Many of the psalm writers memorably expressed their complaints and their anger to God. David frequently asks God how much longer he is going to have to suffer and when God will take this or that affliction from him. In fact, quite a few of God's chosen leaders complained freely. I can imagine Adam asking God, "Why am I all alone? All the animals have another animal to keep them company. How come I have to be all by myself?" Complaining, it seems, is human nature.

But many Christians believe that complaining is bad. They seem to think that God doesn't care about their suffering. One of my friends often says that God is too busy to be concerned about her little problems. She believes God has more important things—like world hunger, for instance—to deal with than her own personal suffering.

If that's true, what about Jesus' statement that God numbers even the hairs of our heads (Matt. 10:30)? Perhaps you don't take that verse literally. Perhaps you think that it means that God knows a great deal about the goings-on in the world, but that God won't necessarily do something about them.

Could be. But I don't believe it. I believe that God does care about the details of our lives—and God especially cares about our suffering.

Even so, it has taken a long time for me to stop feeling guilty about my need to express negative feelings. I was convinced that my need to dwell on how terrible I felt meant I was lacking in some important quality. And because I felt really, really terrible, I spent a whole lot of time lamenting. During the worst periods, I cried a lot. I cried with tears and without tears. I cried out to God and to the people in my life and with the people in my life. I wondered why things were the way they were. I wondered how I was going to survive and why I had survived in the first place. I wondered why I didn't just die.

Part of our need to lament comes from recognizing that life is not what it is supposed to be. No matter who you are, life is difficult some of the time. For some people, it's difficult most of the time. Within the Christian community, there's a lot of emphasis on praise and thanksgiving since Jesus died for us and came back to life. But too often we forget that although Christ won the war, Christians still have many battles to fight. And you and I are fighting those battles every day.

How long do we have to go on fighting our battles? Why doesn't God hear our laments and answer our prayers? Why doesn't God take away our pain? I have no comforting answer to those questions. I believe that God hears our laments and that God suffers with us in our pain. But I also know that sometimes God is terribly, horribly silent. Suffering continues.

I confess that I do not know the workings of God. If I did, God would not be God. But I do know one thing: because of the resurrection of Jesus Christ, I have life. And so do you. Let us allow space and time in that life to express our lament, confident that God will hear us. And continue to love us.

But you, O Sovereign LORD,

deal well with me for your name's sake;

out of the goodness of your love, deliver me.

For I am poor and needy,

and my heart is wounded within me.

I fade away like an evening shadow;

I am shaken off like a locust.

My knees give way from fasting;

my body is thin and gaunt.

Help me, O LORD my God;

save me in accordance with your love.

—Psalm 109:21-24, 26

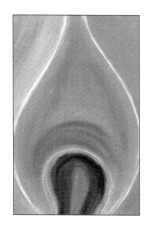

I often had the feeling that something bad was stalking
me. Although I now feel that someone is watching
over me and caring for me, it wasn't always so.

EIGHT
God as Father

Though my father and mother forsake me, the LORD will receive me.

—Psalm 27:10

Father's Day. Mother's Day. Ever since I started dealing with the pain of abuse, I've had trouble with these two Sundays celebrating parenthood. It was difficult for me to honor two people who should have protected me better when I was a child. I had to admit that I was enraged by their failure to do so.

Being failed by your parents is extremely painful. Parents are supposed to know all; they are supposed to be strong and keep evil away from their children. They are the ones we depend on the most. The family is supposed to be safe, and it is the parents' job to make sure that the family stays safe. If you got hurt, your parents failed at doing their job. And the feelings of betrayal are compounded for those who experienced abuse within the family.

Maybe people who want to have children ought to get a license first. Maybe they should be required to pass a test before they are allowed to become pregnant. After all, we make sure that everyone takes classes and passes a test before they're allowed to drive a car. Surely raising a child is at least as much of a responsibility as driving. OK—I'm not really in favor of the Big Brother approach. But I do think people ought to learn a few skills before they decide to bring another human being into this world.

I have to admit something here. If such a test had been in place when I decided to have children, I would have failed miserably. I was a terrible parent in the beginning, and sometimes I'm not sure I've improved all that much. I know a couple who talks about starting a therapy fund along with the college fund for their two children because they are convinced that their parenting is going to drive their children into therapy at some point. But despite our bungled parenting, my children and theirs are a blessing in this world. I guess it's a good thing God doesn't make good parenting a requirement to those who have children.

Although I'm able to forgive myself for my parenting, I must confess that I am not as forgiving when I consider my own mom and dad. I expected them to be perfect, and I expected God to require them to be good parents by the time they had me. I was, after all, their third child. By then, I figured, they should have had plenty of practice.

They weren't perfect. And I allowed their imperfections to block out the image of God as Father. You can't sit though a church service without hearing about God the Father, and some Christians can't even have a conversation without referring to God the Father. Trouble is, the image of God as Father is intolerable if a father or any male authority figure has abused you.

I had already decided that I could do quite well without parents, thank you very much. And I could do quite well without God too. It's all very nice to be given life, I thought, but now that you've sent me on my way, I'd really appreciate it if you could just leave me alone.

I am like the two people walking to Emmaus after the death of Jesus. They believed wholeheartedly that Jesus was going to save them from their miserable lives under the rule of the Romans. Jesus was everything to them, just as my parents were everything to me when I was a child. All their hope of deliverance from the Romans was invested in the kingship of Jesus, just as all my hope for deliverance from abuse was invested in my parents. When my parents failed to protect me, my hope of salvation died. Like the two men from Emmaus, I walked away—disappointed, downhearted, hopeless, confused, and tired—from a dream of perfection.

Then Jesus met the two walkers on the road. Without recognizing him, they explained that their whole world had just come crashing down around their heads. Everything they had hoped for was gone. Jesus told them that they were confused. They had the wrong expectations. Their hope should not be, after all, in the things of this world. Things were not as they seemed to be. The end had not come. They were not alone.

Like the disciples on the road to Emmaus, I have spent a lot of time explaining to God how my whole world came crashing down around me. See God, I say, let me tell you how things were supposed to work. I was supposed to have a long and happy marriage, four children, a house, a yard, a car or two, a husband who makes a good living, and my health. But that's not what I have. I am a divorced mother of two children. I live in an apartment with a small yard and I earn small wages from odd jobs, but mostly I'm supported by the government and by my parents.

In response, I have been getting a consistent, clear, and persistent message: God is sufficient for me. God is to be my all.

I am not very happy with this idea. I am like a spoiled little girl who digs her heels in and refuses to be taken to the ice cream store because she is angry that she couldn't go to the ice cream store yesterday. If I couldn't have it then, I don't ever want it.

But God gently calls to me again, reminding me that God is sufficient in all things. I do not need my parents to protect me anymore. I do not need to put my hope in the things of this world. Life is not as it appears to be. My parents failing me as a child is not the end. I am not alone. And I need to let go of my wrong expectations. God is not going to save me from the disappointments of my life. I will not suddenly have all that I had hoped to have. But if I can let go of my parents' imperfections and my own wrong expectations, I can embrace God's offer to be all that I need.

Thinking of God as Father is not a requirement. But it's a comfort if you can believe that God will give you all that your earthly father couldn't.

God ahead, God behind

God be on the path I wind

God above, God below

God be everywhere I go

God in the steep

God in the shade

God me safe keep

Come to my aid.

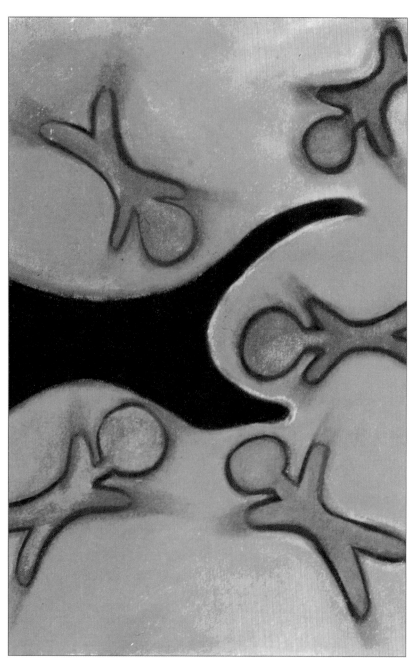

On occasion, I felt that I was the only one under the black hand, but in truth there were others beside me. Some walked the road with me; others suffered similar pain; a few suffered because I was suffering.

Going It Alone

*Then he said to them, "My soul is overwhelmed with sorrow to
the point of death. Stay here and keep watch with me."*
—Matthew 26:38

Today is Memorial Day. I'm home alone with no plans. No one has
invited me to a barbecue. My children are with their father in
another state, and my friends in the neighborhood are at parties of
other friends. To top it off, my closest family and our family grave-
yard is three hundred miles away, so I have no relatives, dead or
alive, to visit. Don't get me wrong—I chose to be alone on this par-
ticular day. I wanted to write without interruption. And being alone
is familiar, sometimes even easy for me. Even so, spending a holi-
day by myself brings back some of the crushing feelings I sometimes have about being alone.

When I am alone, I think that there isn't one person who is available, willing, or interested in being with me or caring about me.
Even my therapist, who has been with me through some of the
worst moments in the past years, is suspect because I pay him, so
of course he acts in a caring fashion toward me. (Those who say that
money can't buy you love clearly don't know about therapy.)

If God intended for me to be alone, I don't believe that I would find
the experience so crushing. My heart yearns for companionship, for
love, for affection, for interaction with others. Even God's own Son,

Jesus, had the disciples to keep him company. And he needed them. When he was agonizing in the garden of Gethsemane before his crucifixion, he begged the disciples to watch and pray with him. At one point, he finds them sleeping and cries out, "Could you men not keep watch with me for one hour?" (Matt. 26:40).

In the face of my yearning for companionship, however, the wound in my heart warns me against seeking people out. *Remember your hurt,* my scarred heart whispers. *It was people you loved and trusted who hurt you and stole from you.* So I often choose to remain alone. In those moments, the fear of injury remains greater than the desire for community.

It's no surprise that when I started my long journey toward healing, I believed that I would walk alone. I was sure that healing was something I'd have to accomplish all by myself. I couldn't imagine that even one person would be willing to accompany me on the smallest part of the journey. If people noticed me at all, I thought they'd merely stand on the shoulder of the road, watching me struggle by.

Someplace along the line I needed to take a leap of faith. Despite my experiences, I needed to believe that someone, maybe just one person, would be there to help me.

The first time I encountered such a person was at the point when I was incapable of driving to my therapy appointments. I was too sick. Either I would have to ask someone to drive me there or not go. So I asked a friend for help. Each time I asked, she agreed to drive me. But it wasn't until the third or fourth time that I finally realized she wasn't standing on the side watching; instead, she was walking down the road with me. It was an epiphany.

If you're ever convinced that you are meant to be alone, consider Adam and Eve. God said, "It is not good for the man to be alone. I will make a helper suitable for him" (Gen. 2:18). Voila, God created Eve. Finding community isn't usually quite that simple, but the statement is still valid—it is not good for any man or woman to be alone.

I have learned—and am still learning—that I am not going to heal all by myself. The road to healing is difficult and dangerous. It is filled with pitfalls, traps, overwhelming fear, and paralyzing darkness. I am not going to make it on my own. If I am going to travel any further along this road, I must let others into my life. Without the help of friends, all those dangerous places would halt me completely. As it is, I still get bogged down, but then someone steps forward and pulls me out.

It has taken literally countless interactions of people picking me up when I fall down for me to begin to believe that people can help, not just hurt. *Begin* to believe. I still have trouble with this. I was telling a friend how I was dreading the final detail work of pulling this book together. She suggested that perhaps I could ask someone to do that for me. Immediately a small voice popped into my head to say that *of course* no one would be willing to do that. Who would possibly want to do that for me? I found myself back at the beginning. So let me say it again: the road to healing is difficult. And I begin the journey along that road by asking for help.

One of my friends once told me that I don't pretend to have it all together. People who know me, he said, know where I stand and what I need because I am always asking for help. That's not so much a glowing endorsement of my character as a reflection of just how much help I need. But I don't believe I need any more help than others do in similar situations. The difference is not so much in the need as in the asking.

I don't mean to suggest that by asking you will get all of your needs met. Or that because I'm not afraid to ask for help, I am completely fulfilled. The reality is that I have lots of unmet needs, and people who can meet those needs are not always available. That was true for the Son of God as well—the disciples still fell asleep even after Jesus asked them to stay awake. You and I know that there is no perfection in this world. But that doesn't mean it's not worth asking for help. Unless I ask, I will certainly be alone. No one is going to come and save me. No one is going to show up on my doorstep to offer help if they don't know I need help.

Being alone can be familiar. It can even sometimes be easy. But it does not bring healing.

Turn to me and be gracious to me,

for I am lonely and afflicted.

The troubles of my heart have multiplied;

free me from my anguish. . . .

Do not turn me over to the desire of my foes,

for false witnesses rise up against me,

breathing out violence.

I am still confident of this:

I will see the goodness of the Lord

in the land of the living.

—Psalm 25:16-17; 27:12-13

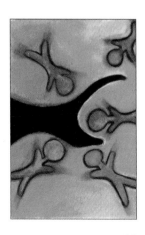

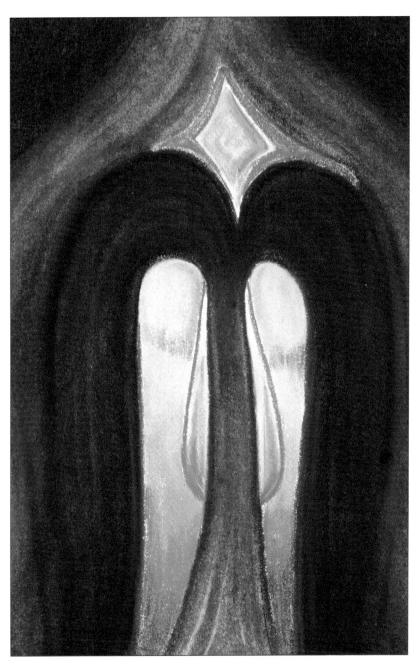

This was a picture of my depression. I am the dropping-to-the-ground "tree" with the light always unattainable behind me. But my mother calls this the "Bethlehem star" picture, depicting the promise of hope and salvation.

TEN
What About Hope?

But those who hope in the LORD
will renew their strength.
They will soar on wings like eagles;
they will run and not grow weary,
they will walk and not be faint.
—Isaiah 40:31

I brought a hand-sized rock with the word *hope* engraved in it to my therapist's office. He keeps it on the windowsill, although he might have to put it away sometimes, he says, if he thinks another client will see it as a weapon. I could relate—there are times during my sessions when I feel a strong urge to hurl the rock through the glass window. I can easily picture the rock shattering the glass with a great splintering sound. In fact, it would be incredibly gratifying to break the glass with my hope.

Very early in my journey I pictured myself trapped behind glass. Part of me—the person walking around, interacting with the world—could see the other part of me behind the glass, but I couldn't touch her, speak to her, or free her. She was the part of me who hurt, who cried, who felt pain. For many years I denied her existence. I made her absolutely silent; she was visible only to me.

The idea that I should find hope in the idea of pitching hope out the window is somewhat paradoxical. Let me explain: the hope I grew up with is not the hope I have today. When I was a child, I hoped that someone would come and rescue me. I hoped that this horrible thing wasn't happening to me. And I clung to those hopes far into adulthood. I found it difficult to let them go. Difficult to pitch them out the window.

But that kind of hope was inevitably crushed. The reality was that no one did come to help. And, no matter how hard I tried, I couldn't change what had happened to me. My hope for a "normal" life had to die if I were to go on living. The experience of abuse is etched indelibly into my life. I will not suddenly become undamaged and completely whole. All of my experiences, whether painful or joyful, make me who I am today; they are part of who I am.

Sometimes I wonder how I have survived and how am I going to keep on surviving. Where am I going to find the strength, the courage, the will, the drive, the energy to put one foot in front of another for one more minute, one more hour, one more day? Because some days, all I really want to do is go home, get under the covers, and go to sleep.

The verse in Isaiah at the beginning of this chapter addresses this struggle to go on, to take one step at a time. Isaiah uses the image of a wilderness to address a people whose sinfulness made their lives a weary struggle instead of a joyful pilgrimage. The desert is a place of extremes—a place where the lack of water makes travel dangerous, yet a place of great beauty.

Flying is an image of great freedom and power. But most of us can't fly. Running through a desert is a grueling task requiring great stamina and strength—something many of us do not have. On the other hand, given enough time and the right supplies, most of us could probably walk through a desert. Walking is for people who don't have a great deal of strength. Compared to flying and running, walking is for the young, the old, the slow, and the weak. Most people can't fly or even run, but they can walk. I can walk. Most of the time.

At times, though, I can't even walk. And then I realize just how much help I need from God. This is a difficult thing to admit. I'd like to believe that I have enough strength and that I have made it this far because I have worked so hard. Sometimes I am strong. And I have worked hard. But I couldn't have come to this point without God. Isaiah doesn't say that those who have a lot of stamina will walk or run or fly. No, he says, "those who hope in the LORD" will soar and run and walk.

What does it mean to put your hope in the Lord? After all, you probably did put your hope in God at some point in your life. Maybe not now but someplace along the way, you cried out for God to save you. And you didn't get saved. So what's the point of putting your hope in God?

I can only speak for myself. Putting my hope in God is to believe, to trust that I will find the courage to put one foot in front of another. I cannot change the past, and I don't have a great deal of control over the future. I was not saved from being abused, nor am I being miraculously healed from it. But right now, in this moment, I can choose to move. And every step that I take brings me closer to the other side of the desert.

Perhaps you wonder if I don't have bigger plans for my life. Don't I hope to have enough money to retire comfortably or to own a house, or that my children will grow up happy and healthy? I won't deny wanting some of those things. I dream big; I expect great and glorious things to come my way. But I hope small because small gets me where I want to go.

I am weak and frail most of the time. I am frightened and lonely much of the time. But I can take one more step and then another. Maybe walking will become easier, maybe not. Regardless, I am walking, and I have hope. Because God is with me. Even in the middle of the desert.

Lord, the sea is so large

And my boat is so small

—Prayer of the Breton fishermen